EDWARDIAN GOWER
REVISITED

EDWARDIAN GOWER REVISITED

David Gwynn

and

Peter Muxworthy

GOMER

First Impression — October 1994

ISBN 1 85902 153 0

Printed and Published by
Gomer Press
Llandysul, Dyfed
Wales

ACKNOWLEDGEMENTS

We would like to thank the following for their invaluable help:

Mrs Joan Davies; Mr Ernest Smith; Mr Clive Johns; Mrs Llinos Johns; Mr George Edwards; Mrs Valerie Mumby; Mrs Barbara Grove; Dr Mark Vernon-Roberts; Mr Edward Harris; Mr Walter Grove; Mr Christopher Beynon; Glamorgan County Archives—West Glamorgan Search Room; The Gower Society; Mr Walter Gwynn; Mr Doug Davies; Mr Donald Jenkins; Mrs Alicia Gwynn.

PREFACE

Our first book, *A Pictorial Journey through Edwardian Gower*, proved to be a great success. Since its publication in 1988, we have gathered together more interesting pictures of Gower during the early years of this century. Therefore, we have decided to produce a second book.

In the first book, we treated the Edwardian period with some flexibility, including illustrations dating from the late nineteenth century and from the 1920s and 1930s. Once again we have adopted a flexible approach, as it allows us to include a number of interesting images, and yet remain loyal to the period in question.

This time we are able to reproduce two paintings by Edward Duncan RWS, as well as more paintings by his son Edward Duncan Jnr and sketches by his grand-daughters, the Misses Duncan of Horton. Also, we feel privileged to be able to include some paintings by James Harris, a renowned painter of seascapes. As far as we know, these have not been published elsewhere. Similarly, most of the photographs reproduced have not been published elsewhere.

INTRODUCTION

This, our second pictorial journey through Edwardian Gower, will hopefully reflect the mix of activities which were an integral part of life on the peninsula during this period of great change.

Tourism in Gower was of little importance prior to the turn of the century. However, improvements in transportation, and a greater willingness on the part of the local people to accommodate visitors, led to a boom in tourism in the years before the First World War and during the inter-war years.

Whilst the tourists came to visit the beaches and picturesque villages, Gower folk carried on with their own business. Agriculture was the mainstay of the local economy, together with fishing, quarrying and, at Llanmorlais and Penclawdd, coal mining. There were several large houses—Stouthall, Kilvrough, Parc le Breos, Fairyhill and Penrice Castle—where a few local people found work, with more being employed outdoors on the estates. Penrice Estate was probably the largest single employer, although each of the estates needed a goodly number of hands in order to function.

Gower folk also were concerned to have their children educated, carry out their religious observance, enjoy some leisure when time allowed, and to cope with the unexpected happenings that fate would ordain from time to time. All of these various activities are depicted in this book.

A SECOND PICTORIAL JOURNEY THROUGH EDWARDIAN GOWER

The first illustration in this book is in the form of a map of Gower, a postcard published before the First World War. In addition to peninsular Gower, the map also shows Swansea, the Swansea Valley as far north as Pontardawe, Llanelli and the Carmarthenshire coast as far west as Kidwelly. A closer look reveals how much detail has been included in a small space. All the railway lines are shown, including the Mumbles Railway and the main line from Swansea Victoria Station which travelled up Clyne Valley to Killay and Dunvant and thence to Gowerton. Also shown is the branch line from Gowerton to Penclawdd and Llanmorlais. On the peninsula, all the villages are marked, including farms and houses that a modern map would not mention. Try to spot, by way of example, Gander Street, High Newton and Bush Park.

The Mumbles Railway is world famous, and in its heyday it carried thousands of people along the shore of Swansea Bay to Mumbles and back. At Mumbles, the main attractions were the pier, from which pleasure steamers departed on trips, and Mumbles Head, a popular spot for a walk, a picnic, and to take in the views of Swansea Bay, the Mumbles lighthouse and the broad expanse of the Bristol Channel. Just beyond Mumbles Head and the lighthouse on the islets, Bracelet Bay was another popular attraction made easily accessible by the Mumbles Railway.

Partnered with Bracelet Bay, between Mumbles Head and Rams Tor, is Limeslade Bay. This was the site of an ancient iron-ore mine, which had been worked from Roman times up to its final closure in 1890. Following the demise of mining, albeit small scale, Limeslade was also ready to accept visitors. It had the advantage of being only a short walk from the Mumbles Pier terminus of the Mumbles Railway, and also being at the end of the coast-hugging road from Swansea. At Limeslade, the road turns inland to avoid the promontory of Rams Tor. The shallow valley at Limeslade allowed development that was not possible at Bracelet, situated at the foot of Mumbles Hill. The break in development after Southend gave Limeslade a certain cachet, and in the years following the First World War, many chalet-style bungalows were built there. Some were occupied year-round; others, however, were only used as holiday homes. In recent years, the pace of development at Limeslade has quickened, although the road inland remains largely unaltered, being narrow in places.

For the foot traveller, the path around Rams Tor allows access to Gower's coast, while the motorist must negotiate the lanes to Newton. Here, the Edwardian traveller would have found a tranquil Gower village, despite its proximity to Mumbles and Swansea. In the village lived many 'donkey-boys' who would wait at the Mumbles Railway station at Oystermouth to bring trippers through Newton and down to Langland and Caswell Bays. Newton was also, for a short time, the home of the nineteenth-century hymn writer Frances Ridley Havergal, who died in 1879.

Langland Bay, its tiny sister Rotherslade, and Caswell Bay are all accessible from Newton and even before the growth of tourism during the early years of the present century, were all popular with trippers from Swansea. Traditionally, Caswell was both Swansea's last bay and Gower's first, for the boundary between Swansea Borough and Gower Rural District divided the bay.

We began our first pictorial journey through Edwardian Gower at Caswell, but on this occasion we felt it more appropriate to set off at Mumbles, which many people see as a gateway to Gower, and then proceed to Murton, with views of Northway and Holt's Field. On this journey we will also visit a number of churches. Some have remained unaltered over the years but others such as Bishopston Church, which was restored in 1851 and again in 1927, bear the signs of considerable change.

The walker leaving Caswell on the coastal path will pass Brandy Cove and Sevenslades before arriving at the bottom of the Bishopston valley at Pwll-du Bay. This bay rang to the noise of limestone quarrying in the nineteenth century, but Edwardian visitors would have found a peaceful, remote place. Refreshments were also available at the Beaufort Inn, a hostelry formerly patronised by the quarrymen. The very seclusion of the bay, and the fact that proper vehicular access was (and indeed still is) impossible, meant that such places could not

survive. Jenkins' Tea Rooms did, however, continue to provide succour into the inter-war years.

Parkmill has long been a gathering place for the local inhabitants of south Gower. In addition to the Gower Inn and the New Inn, there was also a post office, sawmill, a school and a police station. Young people from Pennard, Ilston, Penmaen, and even further afield, would meet at Parkmill to talk, to drink and maybe to indulge in a little tomfoolery. At Parkmill, also, two streams meet to form the Pennard Pill, which flows to the sea at Three Cliffs Bay. One stream—called the 'Killy-Willy' by some former inhabitants—runs down Ilston Cwm, flows between the Gower Inn and the school, and then takes a sharp right-hand turn by the forge and runs alongside the road past New Inn to the mouth of Green Cwm. Here it meets the second stream, which flows from Llethrid past Giant's Grave and the mill. The united stream heads for the sea, under the ruined walls of Pennard Castle.

On our first journey, we visited Ilston Cwm but not Ilston itself. As today, Ilston in the Edwardian era was a small community, isolated by narrow lanes, yet busy owing to the presence of a large limestone quarry just to the north of the village. Beyond the quarry lies Fairwood Common, and the 'north road' from Killay to Llanrhidian. The Ilston stream traverses this common, and the north road crosses it at nearby Cartersford. We, however, must follow our Edwardian traveller along the south road.

Heading westward he would pass the lodge of Parc le Breos house, and arrive at Penmaen. Here, in the church dedicated to St John, is a memorial which harks back to the pre-Norman history of Gower. It reads, 'Here resteth the Body of David the sonne of David the sonne of Richard the sonne of Nicholas the sonne of Rys the sonne of Leison the sonne of Rys the sonne of Morgan Ychan the sonne of Morgan the sonne of Cradocke the sonne of Iustin ap Gwrgan sometime Lord of Glamorgan interred the 21st day of August in the yeare of our blessed redemption 1623'.

From Penmaen, tracks give access to Three Cliffs Bay and Tor Bay. Alongside the track to Tor Bay can be found a megalithic passage grave and Penmaen Old Castle, whose Norman motte was erected for temporary defence whilst the conquerors consolidated their position in the area.

We have included several paintings of the Great Tor, Three Cliffs Bay and Pennard Castle. There are paintings by Edward Duncan Jnr, James Harris and an unidentified member of the Vivian family. Although we risk being accused of repetition, it is fascinating to note the contrasting styles and different interpretation of the same subject matter. The paintings of Pennard Castle, especially, allow comparison over a thirty year period.

From Tor Bay one can appreciate the expanse of Oxwich Bay. To reach the bay by road, however, involves travelling a few miles along the south road before turning left at the Towers. The lane to Oxwich begins with Underhill and then bridges the Pill, a small stream that flows through the Millwood at Penrice, passes below Penrice Castle and then meanders across the sands of Oxwich Bay.

At Oxwich we venture inside another church. Oxwich church is very old, some authorities claiming it to have been built on the site of a sixth-century Celtic hermit's cell. According to legend, the font was brought to the site by St Illtyd, to whom the church is dedicated.

A regular visitor to Oxwich in the 1920s and 1930s was Dame Lilian Bayliss, who was the director of the Old Vic in London. Whilst on her annual holidays, she would sometimes stay with Canon and Mrs de Boinville at the vicarage. Mrs de Boinville was very keen on introducing local girls to cultural activities, such as singing and dancing, and on occasions Dame Lilian would be persuaded to give dancing or drama lessons to her 'girls'. Dame Lilian was a philanthropist, often bringing ill or poor young artists to Oxwich for a holiday. On one occasion, one of her protégés expressed his thanks by painting the ceiling of the chancel of the little church so loved by his patron. Dame Lilian, of course, paid for the materials!

Another story associated with the church at Oxwich might better belong to the domain of legend were it not for the quality of the witnesses. The story was recorded by the Rev. J. D. Davies, the greatest of Gower's prelate antiquarians. He was rector of Cheriton and Llanmadoc and wrote four volumes on the history of Gower, each filled with gems of information. J. D. Davies was born in Oxwich Rectory, his father being the local rector. The event he relates was witnessed by his father and brother:

My oldest brother, now deceased, when a lad of about thirteen or fourteen years of age, had been out one evening with my father fishing in the bay. It was late when they landed, and by the time they had finished mooring the boat, it was nearly twelve o'clock. They had just gained the top of the beach, which here abuts the narrow path leading to the church, when my brother happened to look behind him, saw what he described to me to be a white horse walking on his hind legs and proceeding leisurely along the path to the church gate; having called my father's attention to this strange spectacle, he turned round for about a minute, and watched the creature, or whatever it was, until it reached the gate, or rather the stone stile by its side, which the animal crossed, apparently without the slightest difficulty, still going on its hind legs. The uncanny thing then disappeared. The only remark my father made was 'come along'. They were soon inside the rectory, which was only a few yards off. The strange adventure was never afterwards spoken of by my father, nor alluded to in any way. I have often been on the point of questioning him about it, but some vague feeling of undefined alarm always prevented me!

A tradition does exist amongst Gower folk of the 'Water Kelpie', a white horse-like creature said to emerge occasionally from the spuming surf. It seems that there have been other, sometimes more dramatic, appearances at Oxwich, but this one was unusual in being witnessed by two sober, upstanding citizens.

Before leaving Oxwich, it is worthy of note that the first aeroplane flight in Wales took place on Oxwich beach on 19 January 1911. Mr E. Sutton succeeded in making a short flight some 20-30 feet above the sand in his Bleriot monoplane.

The Edwardian visitor, like his modern-day counterpart, could look northward from Oxwich Bay and see on the skyline the outline of Penrice village. This ancient settlement was at one time the very heart of Gower, with twice-weekly markets and an annual fair. It is likely that only the most intrepid Edwardian travellers would have ventured to Penrice. The village was—and indeed still is—rather isolated, yet to the antiquarian, Penrice has many attractions.

Just outside the village, alongside the lane to Horton, a farmhouse called Sanctuary stands testament to the area's medieval religious history. The Edwardian traveller would not only have encountered a working farm but also a large and ancient farmhouse originally built by the Order of St John, whose South Wales headquarters were at Slebech in Pembrokeshire. Buildings similar to Sanctuary were erected in convenient places and were used as accommodation and offices and from time to time members of the Order would visit such establishments in order to gather their dues and keep an eye on their interests.

In Penrice, visitors could see the pound, where stray animals were held until claimed; the base of the old village cross, and 'The Mount'. All of these features can still be seen, although both the pound and 'The Mount' are now somewhat overgrown. In fact, 'The Mount' is the oldest structure in the village, for it was built by the first Norman lord of Penrice, as the base of a wooden castle he erected for his own protection in those early, uncertain years following the Norman conquest. Subsequently, a great stone castle was built about half a mile away and 'The Mount' was abandoned.

The church at Penrice was probably begun very late

in the eleventh century, and internal features show evidence of the involvement of an immigrant Saxon mason.

The lane—Deep Lane—from the village to the mill and the castle descends the hill behind the church. At the bottom of the hill, the Edwardian traveller would have had a clear view of the Georgian mansion built in 1774 by Sir Christopher Rice Mansel Talbot and seen the ruins of the mill built by a man called Bennet in the middle of the sixteenth century. Ahead, the lane climbs a steep hill called 'Penny Hitch' before joining the main south road at the Home Farm. Many years ago an enterprising fellow—possibly related to the miller—would hire out a horse for one penny to help both people and loads up the hill, hence 'Penny Hitch'.

At the Home Farm, the Edwardian visitor would have seen somewhat a different sight from today. At that time the farmhouse was thatched and the small smithy would have been in operation. The famous granary, which stands on mushroom-shaped legs, has not changed. Probably built early in the nineteenth century, this granary is thought to be the oldest of its type in Wales.

Just a short distance along the south road a lane leads the traveller to Eynonsford. It is here, in this tiny community, that the 'Verry Folk' made one of their occasional appearances, an event again recorded for posterity by the Rev. J. D. Davies:

One memorable night, after all the inmates had gone to bed, Mr S., the tenant of Eynonsford, thought that he dreamt that the 'Verry folks' were on his premises, he fancied too in his dream, that he heard a very faint sound of soft and sweet music, and the light patter of feet, as of people dancing. After a while he awoke, and lo, it was not a dream, but a reality, and he beheld a sight which so overwhelmed him with astonishment, that he was, as it were, spellbound, and could neither speak nor move. Being quite wide awake, he saw the cowstall filled with a multitude of the 'Verry folks', too many to count, gambolling about apparently in great good humour, their attention being particularly directed to one fine fat ox that was quietly chewing the cud by his accustomed post; along his broad back these little creatures, about a foot high, swarmed in scores, while every now and then a couple of them would spring high in the air, and alighting with one foot upon the points of the animals horns, would then spin round with such swiftness that it almost made him giddy to look at them, meanwhile those on the back of the ox were engaged in dancing, continually changing their steps, and keeping the most perfect time to the music of the fiddle played by one of the company. Occasionally in their gambols these diminutive little fellows, all dressed in scarlet and green, would kick off the caps from each others heads, a performance that seemed to afford much amusement. After observing them for some time, Mr S. stated that he gradually got the better of his previous alarm, and waited with the greatest interest for the end of this strange scene, but strange as it had been, it was nothing to what he was about to see. All at once there was a sudden pause in the general hilarity, and he perceived with some consternation, that they were evidently making preparations for slaughtering the ox; he had a great mind to protest against this part of the proceedings, but, like a wise man, he kept perfectly still, and waited. Sure enough they killed the ox, skinned it, and hung it up on one of the cross beams, all being done with the utmost skill, no butcher could have done it better. This done, they set to work and ate it all up. Mr S. was amazed, not only at the cleverness displayed by the little people, but also at their capacity for eating: to be sure there were thousands of them, for the whole range of buildings appeared to be alive with them from one end to the other. Well, thought Mr S. to himself, there is an end to my fat ox at any rate; not a bit of it, never was such a night of wonders, never perhaps did mortal man ever see such a succession of wonderful things performed by the 'Verry folks' as he did, in the cowstall of Eynonsford on that occasion. When the feasting was over, what did those kind little people do, but collect the bones, but not all, for there was one small bone belonging to one of the legs of the ox which they could not find, and the loss of it seemed to cause them the greatest vexation and dismay; some of them sat down and hid their heads in their hands, others clapped their hands upon their heads, and tore their hair as if they were mad, other gesticulated violently, throwing their arms about in the wildest manner; and if ever there was a time when the 'Verry folks' made use of vehement not to say unscriptural language it was then, the confusion as Mr S. said, was 'beyond', and yet the noise was not louder than the ripple of the sea on the sea shore on a fine summer's day; however, there was no help for it, the bone could not be found, and so they had to do the best they could without it, and cleverly they managed; in an incredibly short space of time, the skeleton of the ox, minus this bone, was fitted together, the skin drawn over it, and in a few minutes, the tenant of Eynonsford had the satisfaction to see his ox standing again by post, quietly munching his fodder, and as well as ever.

The next morning, however, when letting out the cattle, he noticed the ox to be a little lame, the lameness being caused by the absence of that small bone, which had caused so much consternation among the 'Verry folks'.

In order to make certain aspects of the story clear, it is as well to point out that Gower farmhouses at the time were long, low buildings, with the cowstall, house and stable all under one roof. The farmer would have slept in a cupboard bed, with a view into his cowstall, as well as into this house, hence his being able to see the events described above, from his bed, and unseen by his visitors. J. D. Davies himself maintains that the last appearance of the 'Verry folks' had been about one hundred years before he recorded the experiences of Mr S. of Eynonsford. This would place the tale no later than the 1780s, and possibly much earlier.

A traveller wishing to move onwards from Eynonsford could either travel to Reynoldston via the tiny community of Little Reynoldston, or continue along the south road past Stouthall, Knelston and Llanddewi to Horton and Porteynon on the coast. In order to visit Horton before Porteynon, the traveller must take a left turn at Moor Corner, and follow the Penrice road to Horton Cross. The area between Penrice, Horton, Moor Corner and Scurlage has a lonely, windswept air about it, especially in autumn and winter. With place-names like Hangman's Cross and Cold Comfort, there is little to alleviate the sense of desolate isolation. During the Edwardian period, the houses scattered across this area, like Old Well, Maryzun (formerly an inn called The Merry Sun) and Brynsil, were all occupied, and the trackways that criss-cross the area would have been well used. The trackway from Hangman's Cross to Slade is sometimes called Cold Comfort, after a field adjacent to it in which can still be seen a ruined building that was formerly an inn. There are some who claim that the occurrence of a name incorporating the word 'Cold' indicates a link with Roman times. The suggestion is that after the Roman legions left, their ruined way stations and inns only offered a cold welcome. Whether this explanation is correct or not, the ruins of the inn alongside this trackway would offer nothing more than cold comfort.

The trackway at Cold Comfort heads south, whereas another easterly-bound trackway called Sheppan Lane leads from Brynsil Cross to Badger's Hole at Oxwich, where it meets the metalled road. North-west from Hangman's Cross, tracks lead past Old Well to Berry and Scurlage. Anyone walking these paths today would be able to imagine, at least in part, what the roads of Gower would have been like before modern road-building methods were developed.

On our first pictorial journey through Edwardian Gower we lingered long at Horton and Porteynon, for both these villages provided the subject matter for many pictures and postcards. The area was popular amongst campers, there being plenty of space for tents within easy reach of the beach, and both villages were popular with amateur artists. It would seem, therefore, that the area had a rather Bohemian atmosphere throughout the 1920s and early 1930s.

The tendency when writing about Porteynon is to concentrate attention on the lifeboat, the disaster of 1916, the Lucases at Salthouse and the rather mysterious Culver Hole. But Porteynon was also famous during its heyday for oysters, limestone, paint ochre and sailing-ship captains.

The coast from Porteynon to Paviland Cave boasts some of the best crabbing grounds in Gower. The shelving rocks, scattered with pools and creeks, are ideal for crabs and lobsters. They also have a deadlier reputation, as the graveyard of many ships. Indeed, the entire coastline of south-west Gower, from Porteynon Point to Worm's Head can be a wild and windswept place. With the seas up on a stormy winter's night, ships passing this stretch of coast not only had to face the hazards of nature, but also the wreckers who wrought havoc in Gower many hundreds of years ago. Beyond Overton, the isolation and difficulty of the coastline allowed the wreckers to operate undisturbed. The ploy was a simple one—to mislead hard-pressed ship's captains into believing that safety was at hand by placing false lights on the cliffs or rocks. Once the ship was wrecked, and the crew despatched, the cargo was available for looting. How widespread the practice was is hard to say, but there is no doubt that it did take place. Nevertheless, it was not entirely approved of by everyone. One story is told of a Rhosili publican's daughter, who, tiring of the loss of life involved, refused to take a lantern onto the cliff. When forced to do so, she chose to sacrifice herself by leaping from the cliff, rather than lure another unsuspecting ship to doom.

Smuggling was another common practice and there are many smuggling tales linked with Gower. Porteynon was something of a centre for the early smuggling trade, to such an extent that at one stage eight excisemen, and with a boat, were stationed at the village. They even had a watch-house on Porteynon Point. Once Porteynon's trade was quelled, Rhosili became Gower's main smuggling centre.

Generally speaking, there are fewer postcards depicting the north-west corner of Gower. In Edwardian times, fewer tourists visited the villages in this area so the demand for postcards was consequently lower. Some commentators look on this part of the peninsula, and Llangennith in particular, as most typical of old Gower but it would be wrong to infer that the people in these villages were ever behind the times or old fashioned in their ways. There is nothing wrong with being slow to abandon tried and tested practices, unless, of course, they can be shown to be inferior.

The largest stream in west Gower, the Burry Pill, traverses the north-west corner of the peninsula, and along its banks stood seven of the thirteen grist (or corn) mills recorded in the western parishes of Gower. From source to mouth, these are: Higher Mill, Middle Mill, Stackpool Mill, Stembridge Mill, Stonemill, Western Mill and Cheriton Mill. The other mills were the Higher Mill and Lower Mill at Llangennith, Higher Mill and Lower Mill at Llanrhidian, Penrice Mill and Pitton Mill. The last named ground only barley and oats.

The Edwardian traveller would have found only Stackpool Mill, the two mills at Llangennith and Middle Mill still operating. Western Mill, Stembridge Mill and Higher Mill on the banks of Burry Pill all closed around the turn of the century, whilst the remainder closed earlier in the nineteenth century. Middle Mill actually survived until 1942.

Llanmadoc Hill, from the top of which the traveller can survey the expanse of Broughton Bay and Whitford Burrows, separates the villages of Llangennith and Llanmadoc. The latter village is strung along a lane called Rattle Street, at the lower end of which is Frog Street leading to Cheriton, and at the top end, the green and the church. At Llanmadoc, the 'Verry Folk' were rather active, for we have two tales to relate. At Cwm Ivy can be seen a flat green space known as the 'Fairies' Dancing Ground'. Once a fellow from the village was foolish enough to step into the ring when the fairies were dancing. His punishment was to have a pitchfork stuck into his foot. After he arrived home he spoke with a wise woman, who advised him to apologise to the 'Verry Folk'. He did as he was told, placing his foot once again into the ring, with the result that his foot was healed.

At Lagadranta, then an isolated farm under Llanmadoc Hill, one representative of the 'Verry Folk' made an appearance one morning in the guise of an old woman. She asked the farmer's wife for the loan of a sieve, immediately arousing the good lady's suspicions, for that implement, it seems, was often used by the 'Verry Folk' for sifting gold. Needless to say, she did not want to upset the 'Verry Folk', so she lent the old woman a sieve. A few days later, the old woman returned the sieve. As it had been willingly lent, she promised the farmer's wife that her largest cask would henceforth never run out of beer, providing she spoke to no one about their meeting. For several weeks, the cask supplied beer unceasingly, but, once the farmer's wife gossiped to a neighbour, the supply came to an abrupt end.

The road from Llanmadoc takes the traveller through Cheriton, past Landimore and Weobley Castle to the junction with the road from

Llangennith at Oldwalls. Near Weobley Castle is Windmill—locally pronounced 'Wimmal'—Farm which may well have been the site of one of the very few windmills built in Gower. Erected sometime between 1543 and 1583 by Anthony Davers, it is mentioned, along with three grist-mills erected during the same period, in contemporary documents.

On reaching Llanrhidian, the traveller arrives at the last village within the boundary of 'Gower Anglicana'—the 'Englishry'. The next communities along the road to Penclawdd are Crofty and Llanmorlais—two separate settlements in Edwardian times but today grown together. Here the coal-seams are to be found in the Carboniferous rocks and the evidence of the industrial revolution appears in the form of a coal-mine and a railway line. Few pictures survive of the branch railway line from Gowerton to Llanmorlais via Penclawdd and today scant remnants exist of its route, or the route of the canal that preceded it.

Cockles, Penclawdd's claim to fame are much better represented pictorially, although the village itself attracted few photographers. The cocklewomen sold most of their catch in Swansea Market, where they were easily recognisable by their garb of striped woollen skirts, aprons, shawls and a flat-topped straw hats on which the pails of cockles would be balanced. Before the railway line was built to Penclawdd, the cocklewomen would walk to Swansea Market via Killay and Olchfa, where, traditionally, they would wash their feet in the stream before going into the town.

The cocklewomen's route would have taken them through Gowerton and Dunvant. Other travellers from Gower could reach Killay from either north or south by crossing Fairwood Common, the roads joining at Upper Killay. The north road is the older of the two, giving access to Three Crosses, Cilonnen, Cartersford, Llethrid, Cilibion and Llanrhidian. At Cilibion, the Red Road could be taken across Cefn Bryn to reach Reynoldston and south Gower.

The south road across Fairwood Common was delineated by a George Eynon, who set off from Kilvrough with his ox-drawn wooden plough and cut a furrow to the north road. He then did an about turn and cut a parallel furrow on his way back. Precisely when this was done we do not know, but the track became popular as an alternative route to Swansea from south Gower, as it avoided the steep hill at Kittle.

TIME OFF

Time to spend on leisure pursuits was a luxury virtually unknown to most Gower folk before the turn of the century. Hard work was the order of the day, with Sunday demanding religious observance. The markets and fairs at Penrice provided some relief, as did the *Gwyliau Mabsant*, or Saint's Days celebrations at Rhosili, Llangennith and Llanmadoc, while Christmas also allowed some time for pleasure. The first holiday of the year, however, saw folk busy in their gardens. Good Friday was traditionally the day when the gardens were prepared for the summer.

We must not suppose, however, that Gower folk did not know how to enjoy themselves, for their sense of fun was unrivalled. Llangennith *Mabsant* was a particularly riotous occasion, when cock-fighting, prize-fighting, ball-games, eating, drinking and general merry-making took over the three days from 4 July.

Llangennith *Mabsant* died out, possibly in the face of disapproval from various ministers of religion, in the middle of the nineteenth century. At Llanmadoc, the *Gŵyl Mabsant* survived, albeit in a much emasculated form, into the present century.

Childhood games were many but only a few survived the end of the Victorian era. 'Inky Pinky' involved a blindfolded child attempting to break carefully placed eggs with the aid of a stick. Another game was 'Duckstone', in which the aim was to knock a small stone from the top of a larger stone, using other small stones.

In the Edwardian Period, and during inter-war years, a few villages, such as Llanrhidian, Oldwalls and Reynoldston, had quoits teams, who played in a local league, called the 'Gower Light Quoits League'. In Llanrhidian the quoits bed, made of blue clay taken from Cefn Bryn just above Stonyford, was located near the church.

Oldwalls seems to have been a particularly sporting village. In addition to a quoits team, it boasted a rugby team before the First World War, and there was a tennis court near the chapel.

Tennis was a particularly popular sport in Gower, especially during the inter-war years. In those days, the game was played by people from widely differing backgrounds. Oxwich had a village tennis club, with a court near 'The Pump'. Today the site is occupied by the village hall.

Cricket was also played in Gower, there being a small pavilion in Porteynon, although no proper pitch. Doubtless other villages were able to raise teams for games on the various greens.

From 1906, Gower folk were also able to take a day off in September to attend the newly established Gower Agricultural Show which superseded the Gower Fat Stock Show formerly held at Christmas time, and the Gower Flower Show. It did not take long for the Gower Agricultural Show to become firmly established as one of the highlights of the social calendar, for as well as the competitive element, it was an opportunity for folk to meet and exchange gossip.

AGRICULTURE

Mention of the Gower Agricultural Show brings us neatly to the farming life of Gower.

Regrettably, however, very few pictures exist of farming practices in Gower during the early years of the twentieth century although we are able to reproduce a few in this volume, thanks to the foresight of the Greening family of Killay, who had many of their activities recorded on film.

The Greenings were owners of traction engines, so were hauliers as well as agricultural contractors.

Those pictures of threshing in Gower are rather posed but they do give a good idea of the number of people required to get the job done. Greening's traction engines were also pressed into service for more pleasurable activities, such as Sunday School outings. However a major part of Greening's business was concerned with the salvage of shipwrecks, and this in turn brings us to another aspect of Gower in Edwardian times.

SOME GOWER SHIPWRECKS

Many a vessel has been wrecked on the Gower coast but it is not our intention to list them here. For information relating to the wrecks the reader should consult George Edmunds's book *The Gower Coast*. It is appropriate, however, to provide some background information relating to the pictures of those wrecks featured in this book.

The s.s. *Tyne*, bound for Santos from London via Swansea, collided in heavy fog with the French schooner *Fleur de Mer*. After picking up the survivors, the *Tyne* herself went off course and ran aground on the rocks at Langland Bay. At low tide, however, the crew members were able to walk ashore and the vessel itself was subsequently refloated and taken to Swansea to be repaired.

The s.s. *Epidauro* went aground at Washslade Bay, Overton, on 13 February 1913 and became a total wreck. During that period the vessel was comprehensively photographed.

The French steamer s.s. *Tours* ran aground at Deepslade, Pennard, in thick fog in 1919. Again the Greenings were involved in the salvage of the wreck and a number of photographs were taken.

Another wreck with which the Greenings were involved was the s.s. *Fellside*, which ran aground at Heatherslade Bay on 8 January 1924. Greening purchased the wreck, cut it up and sold it for scrap. We are able to reproduce not only a picture of the ship aground, but also two letters relating to the salvage. The first, dated 28 January 1924, is the offer by Greening to purchase the wreck and cargo (the 'pitt wood' referred to is the cargo of pit props). The second is the reply from the agents accepting the offer. It can be seen from the second letter that the offer for the cargo was amended in a telephone conversation subsequent to the first letter being sent.

EDUCATION

Prior to 1870 there was little educational provision in Gower, but as a result of the Education Act of that year, schools were opened in most villages. The three pictures we are able to reproduce in this book are of Oxwich schoolchildren in 1912, Porteynon school children in 1920 and Llanrhidian schoolchildren in 1928. We are able to identify those on the Porteynon school photograph, and a few of those on the Llanrhidian school photograph, but none of those who attended at Oxwich school.

PHIL TANNER

Most areas have celebrities—local boys or girls who have gone on to become nationally or internationally famous in their chosen field. Some become household names. Gower has few such famous sons or daughters. Edgar Evans, to whose memory a tablet stands in Rhosili church is, perhaps, the most famous son of Gower. His bravery as a member of Captain Scott's Antarctic expedition will ensure his place in the annals of history.

Phil Tanner, on the other hand, enjoyed local fame as a folk singer and was fortunate to live long enough to be lauded as a master in that field. Consequently, his name is remembered not only by Gower folk, but also by folk-music enthusiasts world-wide.

Born on 16 February 1862, into a long-established weaving family in Llangennith, Phil's youth was spent in that business. Later, he made the decision to break from weaving and became a farm worker, spending much of his time as a hedger and ditcher. When he was 22 he married Ruth Nicholas, the middle-aged and widowed landlady of the Welcome to Town inn at Llangennith. Following her death in 1921 Phil lived alone at Barraston, about a quarter a mile from the village.

His family were renowned as singers, and Phil learned songs from his father and grandfather. He also picked up new ballads and tunes from others, including the fiddler Tom Lloyd, known as 'Morriston Tom' although he hailed from Mumbles.

Tunes were important to Phil, for he was not just a singer. When the occasion demanded it, he could accompany dancing with 'mouth music'. He knew many tunes but only two have survived, namely 'The Gower Reel' and 'Over the hills to Gowrie'. His repertoire of songs included not only Gower songs, but also a goodly number of Victorian ballads.

Phil had also been closely involved with the traditional Gower 'Bidding Wedding' which, regrettably, was replaced by the now more usual style of wedding, around 1905. In a Bidding Wedding, celebrations would begin a fortnight before the appointed day, which was always a Thursday. Throughout those two weeks, home-brewed ale would be freely available to the villagers. The 'Bidder' would tour the houses in the locality, bidding everyone to come to the wedding and to be generous with their gifts. It seems that Phil Tanner particularly enjoyed this role. On the wedding day, the couple would be married in church and then, in procession, make their way back to the house. At the church gate, children would have tied a rope across the way and the couple would have to throw pennies for them before they were allowed to go on their way.

At the wedding feast, the Bidder approached each guest with two plates on which were placed money contributions for the newly-weds. He would be accompanied by a man entrusted with the task of entering each contribution into a book. Large contributions would be repaid by the couple when the donor in turn got married, and the call 'heave' would mark these as special gifts.

After the feast, there would be merry-making and dancing well into the night. Phil Tanner would be just as much at home providing the music for these dances as any fiddler.

The late-Victorian period had seen a growth in interest in folk songs, and a number of people were actively collecting tunes and songs. For example, Cecil Sharp's Christmastide visit to Headington Quarry in Oxfordshire in 1899 led to his collecting many Morris dances and tunes that would otherwise have died out. Gower, however, did not enjoy the interest of song collectors until the twentieth century. When the BBC first came to visit Phil Tanner it was 1937, and they recorded a number of songs at Barraston. In April and May 1949 the BBC again were able to record Phil singing, although he repeated some of the songs that had been previously recorded. By this time he had also been living at the Glan-y-Môr Eventide Home in Penmaen for eight years, and his repertoire was far less than the 80 or 90 songs and tunes of his heyday.

It is indeed fortunate that Phil Tanner lived to see the second folk-revival in the 1930s, and that he was recorded before he died in 1950. He thus became a legend outside Gower, and his songs were issued on record again during the third folk revival of the 1960s and 1970s.

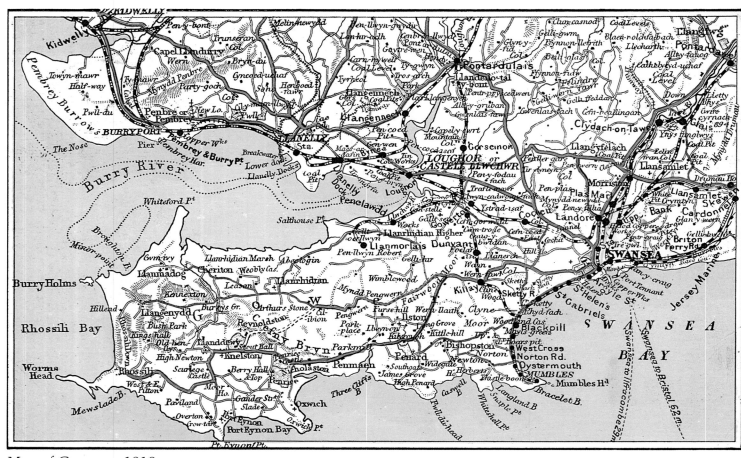

Map of Gower, *c* 1910.

On the way to Mumbles Head from Swansea. The Mumbles train runs through Blackpill.

Mumbles Pier and lighthouse.

Mumbles Head, *c* 1910.

At Bracelet Bay, June 1925.

Bracelet Bay.

Limeslade bungalows, *c* 1935.

Limeslade bungalows, *c* 1935.

St Peter's Church, Newton, *c* 1904.

Newton, Mumbles, *c* 1905.

Newton, Mumbles, *c* 1915.

Newton, Mumbles, *c* 1915.

Newton village, *c* 1915.

Rotherslade, before the promenade was built.

Rotherslade, after the promenade was built.

Langland Bay from the cliff, *c* 1905.

Langland Bay Hotel, *c* 1929.

Caswell Hill, *c* 1910.

Caswell Valley and Bay, Mumbles, *c* 1920.

Caswell Bay, *c* 1926.

Caswell Bay after the storm, 16 December 1910.

Brandy Cove near Caswell Bay.

Northway, Murton, *c* 1923.

Murton, Gower, Holt's Field.

Interior of Bishopston church, *c* 1920.

Old road and new, Kittle, Bishopston, *c* 1930.

Jenkins' Tea Rooms, Pwll-du, *c* 1920.

Parkmill, Gower, *c* 1920.

Parkmill Post Office, *c* 1910.

New Inn Parkmill, *c* 1905.

'Green Cwm' by Edward Duncan Jnr, 1895.

Ilston Church, Parkmill, Gower, *c* 1911.

Wooden bridge over the stream at Ilston, *c* 1905.

'Pennard Castle' by James Harris, *c* 1870.

Pennard Castle. Painting by an unidentified member of the Vivian family, late nineteenth century.

'Pennard Castle' by Edward Duncan Jnr, 1896.

'Three Cliffs—Three People' by James Harris *c* 1870.

The Pill, Three Cliffs Bay, *c* 1905.

Great Tor and Three Cliffs, painted by an unidentified member of the Vivian family, late nineteenth century.

Great Tor from Three Cliffs, painted by an unidentified member of the Vivian family, late nineteenth century.

'Three Cliffs from the Sea' by Edward Duncan Jnr, 1896.

'The Tor' by James Harris, *c* 1870.

Penmaen church and school, *c* 1910.

Nicholaston Hall, Nicholaston, *c* 1915.

The Pill, Oxwich Bay, *c* 1915.

'Cows grazing on Oxwich Marsh' by Edward Duncan Jnr, *c* 1890.

Oxwich Bay, *c* 1910. The large sheds were used to store coal that had been brought into the bay by sea.

'Oxwich Church' by Edward Duncan Jnr, 1896.

Oxwich church interior, *c* 1905.

Oxwich—The Square, *c* 1920.

Woodside cottage, Oxwich, *c* 1908.

Oxwich Post Office, *c* 1920. Notice the charabanc which had probably brought the travellers to Stephens' Tea Rooms.

Oxwich, c 1908. The people are standing outside Box Tree cottage.

Oxwich—a village lane. This view looks north, and Box Tree is the cottage on the left. The residence in the middle distance is Margaret's cottage. This view was probably taken before 1905.

Oxwich. 'The Bank' before it was rebuilt in 1909-10.

Oxwich. 'The Bank' in 1929, some twenty years after it was rebuilt.

'Penrice Castle from the old castle 1900': artist unknown.

Penrice Castle, looking across the lake, *c* 1910.

The Home Farm and Granary, Penrice.

Interior of St George's Church, Reynoldston, *c* 1912.

Reynoldston Hall, 3 March 1924. A fancy dress party by the looks of it. For St David's Day?

Stouthall, Reynoldston, *c* 1912.

Back entrance to Stouthall, Reynoldston, c 1912.

Llanddewi from Knelston, *c* 1924.

LLANDDEWI FROM KNELSTON.
S.B.C.

Llanddewi church, *c* 1905.

82

Moor Corner, *c* 1925. Taking in the hay.

Fernbank, Horton.

Lifeboat and Salthouses, Porteynon,
c 1910.

Salthouse, *c* 1908.

Porteynon lifeboat, 1900: 'A Daughter's Offering'.

Porteynon lifeboat at practice, *c* 1905.

Lifeboat practice, Porteynon, *c* 1913.

Boat scene at Porteynon, *c* 1900.

Campers at Porteynon, *c* 1910.

Campers at Porteynon, *c* 1928.

Postcard inscribed on the reverse 'The Bhoys & the Ghirls' Porteynon, August 1919.

Kite Hole, Overton, 1898. A copy
by M. Duncan of a painting by
A. Duncan.

Overton, Gower *c* 1910.

The 'N's' Cottage, Overton, 1900.

Mewslade. Painting by an unidentified member of the Vivian family, late nineteenth century.

Great Pitton Farm, viewed from the yard *c* 1920. This house is over 500 years old, and is thought to be the oldest continuously inhabited dwelling in Gower. It is now a Grade II listed building, and it is interesting to note that the cupboard bed from the farmhouse is now to be seen in Kennixstone farmhouse at the Welsh Folk Museum, St Fagans.

Great Pitton Farm, viewed from the lane, *c* 1920.

William Gwynne Beynon and Gladys Beynon
outside Great Pitton Farm, *c*1920.

'Middleton' by Edward Duncan Jnr, *c* 1890.

Middleton, *c* 1920.

Middleton Bank, Rhosili, *c* 1910.

'Worm's Head' by Alfred Parkman, *c* 1906.

Interior of St Mary's Church, Rhosili, Gower, *c* 1910.

'Wreckers in Rhosili Bay' by Edward Duncan RWS 1842.

Fall Bay, Rhosili, *c* 1906.

Cathan Farm, Harding's down, *c* 1884. A copy by M. Duncan of a painting by Edward Duncan Jnr.

'Bethesda Chapel Burry Green, Trinity Chapel Cheriton, Zion Chapel Llangennith'; artist and date unknown.

Delvid, Broughton, Llangennith, *c* 1925.

West End, Llangennith, *c* 1920.

Llangennith village, *c* 1910.

The Green, Llangennith, *c* 1925.

'Old Wreck—Llangennith' by Edward Duncan RWS, *c* 1860.

Frog Lane, Llanmadoc, *c* 1918.

Rectory Road, Llanmadoc, *c* 1922.

Post Office, Llanmadoc, *c* 1922.

Measuring the whales at Llanmadoc, 7 May 1934.

Cheriton Church, *c* 1908.

Interior of Cheriton Church, *c* 1905.

Cheriton from the Pill, *c* 1915.

'Weobley Castle' by Edward Duncan Jnr, 1890.

Group at Oldwalls where the roads from Llangennith and Llanmadoc join. We are fortunate that the people in this group are all named, and they are, from the left to right: David John, L. Jones, T. Williams, S. Dunn, Mr Ellis, Clifford Roberts, T. F. Davies, Katie John, Mrs Roberts, Douglas Roberts, Mrs Davies, Mrs Jeffreys, Mrs John, Annie Jane (Pitton Cross), Mrs T. Williams, Gower Davies, Miss Williams (Port Eynon), Ivy and Lily Davies, Will Davies (Llanelli), Rachel John and Miss Williams. Although there is no date, the mode of dress suggests the second half of the 1920s.

Greyhound Inn, Oldwalls, *c* 1920.

Old Walls Road, Llanrhidian, *c* 1930.

Vicarage, Llanrhidian, *c* 1915.

Crofty, Penclawdd, *c* 1915.

Beach, Penclawdd, *c* 1914.

Welsh cockle gatherers.

Boiling cockles at Penclawdd, *c* 1924.

Cocklewomen and a donkey, *c*1880. Painting by an unidentified member of the Vivian family.

Llanyrnewydd church, Penclawdd, c 1910.

Siloam Baptist church, Killay.

Gower's oldest inhabitant, 1905. The card states that she lived through five reigns, having been born in Trafalgar Year, 1805, and is shown making hay in 1905. Unfortunately, she is not named.

Oldwalls quoits team, 1926. Back row: Tom Williams, Austin Grove, Frank Jones, Byron Tucker, George Roberts, Stanley Gordon, Arthur Williams. Front row: Cliff Roberts, Haydn Williams, Jack Jones, Cyril Jeffries, Lennie Williams, Tom Williams Jnr, Harry Thomas, Will Thomas.

Oldwalls rugby team, 1909.

Watching tennis at The Hollies, Horton, before 1914.

Oxwich Tennis Club, 1930.

Porteynon Cricket Pavilion, late 1920s.

Leonard Smith of Norton, Oxwich, at the Gower Show of 1919.

Threshing in Gower, *c* 1908.

A break for food during threshing, *c* 1908.

Ploughing with two horses, *c* 1925.

An engine-driven rip-saw *c* 1920.

A Gower Sunday School outing, *c* 1910.

'Wreck of the *Mercor* at Slade' by Edward Duncan Jnr. George Edmunds states that this ship was wrecked in 1879.

The s.s. *Tyne* at Langland in April 1919.

The *Epidauro* on the rocks at Washslade Bay, Overton, Porteynon, 13 February 1913.

The workers at the wreck of the *Epidauro*.

Picking up the pieces of the *Epidauro*.

Cutting up bars of the wreck.

Boilers of *Epidauro* in the sea, Porteynon.

The last of the s.s. *Epidauro*.

s.s. *Tours* at Deepslade Bay, Gower, 1919.

On the s.s. *Tours* at Gower, 1919.

The s.s. *Fellside* in Heatherslade Bay, Gower, 8 January 24.

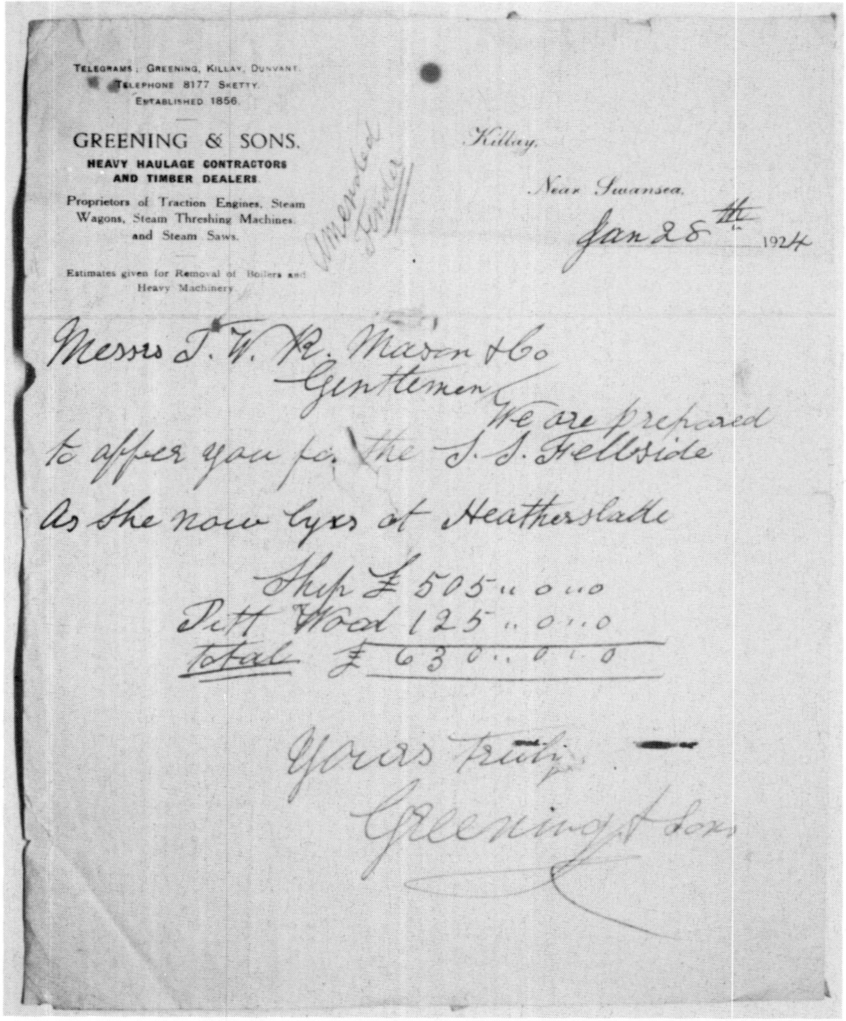

TELEGRAMS: GREENING, KILLAY, DUNVANT.
TELEPHONE 8177 SKETTY.
ESTABLISHED 1856.

GREENING & SONS.
HEAVY HAULAGE CONTRACTORS
AND TIMBER DEALERS.

Proprietors of Traction Engines, Steam Wagons, Steam Threshing Machines and Steam Saws.

Estimates given for Removal of Boilers and Heavy Machinery.

Amended Tender

Killay,
Near Swansea,
Jan 28th 1924

Messrs T. W. R. Mason & Co
Gentlemen,
We are prepared to offer you for the S.S. Fellside
As she now lyes at Heatherslade

Ship £505..0..0
Pitt Wood 125..0..0
Total £630..0..0

Yours Truly
Greening & Sons

Greening's letter regarding the s.s. *Fellside*.

The agent's letter regarding the s.s. *Fellside*.

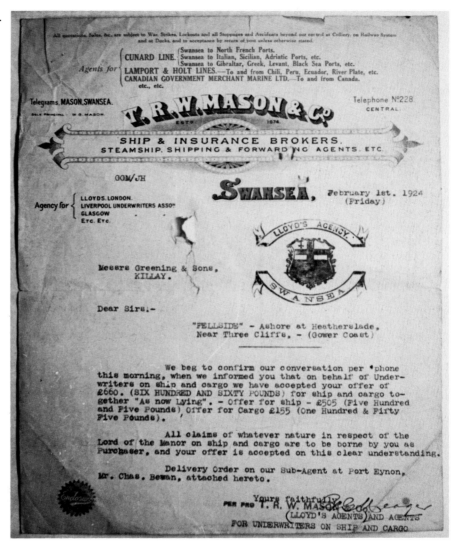

Oxwich School, 1912.

Porteynon School, 1920. Back row, from left: Clifford Howell, Fred Grove, Mollie Jenkins, Vera Rowlands, Milly Phillips, Gladys Johnston, May Stevens. Second row: Archie Jenkins, unknown, Betty Harry, Violet Rheece, Irene Stevens, Trevor Jenkins. Third row: Gladys Thomas, Gwen Tucker, Nora Bevan, Fred Nuttal, Charlie Grove, May Grove, Mary Tucker, Mollie Grove. Fourth row: Eddie Johnston, Albert Nuttal, Frank Bevan, Aubrey Stevens, Will Grove, Albert Grove.

Llanrhidian School, 1928. Far left Miss Cook, with Griff Gwynn next to her, then an unidentified boy, and then Walter Gwynn. The teacher far right is Evan Evans, with Nancy Winch next to him. The fifth pupil from the right in the middle row is Daisy Williams with Dora Beynon the sixth pupil. Glyn Mabbett is the tall boy at the back. The others have yet to be identified.

Phil Tanner.

BIBLIOGRAPHY

J. D. Davies, M.A. *Historical Notices of the Parishes of Penrice, Oxwich, Nicholaston in the Rural Deanery of West Gower*, Swansea, 1894
H. M. Tucker, *Gower Gleanings*, Swansea, 1951
Wynford Vaughan-Thomas, *Portrait of Gower*, London, 1976
George Edmunds, *The Gower Coast*, Bristol, 1979
Glyn Vivian Art Gallery, Swansea City Council, *Under Sail*, Swansea, 1987
Gower (The Journal of the Gower Society), vol I, 1948